Passion, Purpose, and the Pursuit of Happiness

The Journey to Claiming Your Glory

Giovanni Negron-Garcia.

Printed in the United States of America
Copyright © 2022 Giovanni Negron-Garcia

ISBN: 978-0-578-37777-3
Publisher: Giovanni Negron-Garcia

All rights reserved solely by the author. No part of this book may be reproduced, scanned, or distributed in any printed or electronic form without permission.

Edited by Ready Writer Services, LLC

Dedicated to the Negron-Garcia family
and the City of Reading, PA.

Table of Contents

Foreword: Pg. 3

Testimonials: Pg. 5

Preface: Pg. 9

<u>Chapters</u>

1. What is Passion? Pg. 14
2. "Am I Too Passionate?" Pg. 28
3. What is Purpose? Pg. 45
4. Internalizing Your Purpose Pg. 59
5. The Pursuit of Happiness Pg. 73
6. Gifting Yourself a Legacy Pg. 87
7. Claim Your Glory Without Fear Pg. 100

About the Author Pg. 121

Foreword

"Overcoming the odds" is a phrase that is overused by many individuals. The difference between them and Gio could not be more profound. During his childhood, Giovanni was raised in Reading, PA, which is labeled as one of the poorest and most dangerous cities in America. Giovanni attended a school district where most of its students lived below the poverty line and on reduced or free lunch. Walking and playing in streets surrounded by crime and violence. Mr. Negron-Garcia is not the product of his surroundings. Giovanni is humble and comes from a caring Pennsylvanian, Puerto Rican family.

From living in the Reading Public Housing Authority community to becoming a first-generation college graduate on grants and scholarships to dealing with a near death experience because of his poor health, Gio needed no one's validation but his own.

Young Gio could hear the struggles and sacrifices his working-class family was going through and silently prayed for better tomorrows. Rejection almost caused him his health, happiness, and life. At 300 plus pounds, he felt defeated, unwanted, and unworthy.

This book is the finding of your voice, worthiness, and power. This book is about lifting up your city and his own. This book is about the power of self-love. It is about the audacity of young Latino hope.

His faith sustained him through the process of self-discovery, self-respect, and self-reconciliation. Defeating the odds was no casualty as he finds strength from his ancestors to share these words with the world. He is the epitome of the comeback kid.

All I'm saying is never doubt a kid from Reading,
PA. Especially if their name is "Gio" Negron-Garcia.

Norman Bristol Colon
- ❖ Director of Diversity, Equity, and Inclusion
PA Department of Community and Economic Development
- ❖ Chairman of the PA Latino Convention.

Testimonials

"Gio has helped me master what it truly means to take control of your own life. His remarkable support paired with his persistent motivation has given me the initiative to shoot to new heights in my personal and professional career. There is no doubt in my mind that he will help do the same for all the other entrepreneurs (younger or older) out there. Be sure to claim your glory!"

- Carlos Brinkley, Kutztown University Graduate '21

"To be as passionate and driven at a young age is incredible, and Gio has pushed against barriers for me as much as he has for himself. I'll always be grateful to have him as a mentor but even more as a friend."

- Chanaly Rodriguez, Kutztown University Student/ Women's Rights Activist

"Mr. Negron-Garcia is one of a kind. I would love to see our younger generation have the energy and enthusiasm of being such a professional as Mr. Negron-Garcia. Gio has impacted my life by demonstrating what he is capable of! What his life was before and what his life looks like now! Congratulations Gio! You are an inspiration!! I wish you all the best in all your future endeavors! God bless you Gio!"

- Maria Delgado, CEO of Delgado Global Consulting

"I am so excited for Gio because he did not become bitter. God has shown Gio how to use his intelligence to be fruitful and to multiply. I'm a youth leader and I can see Gio helps heal brokenness. Mr. Negron-Garcia is going to build bridges."

- Lynda Joice, Vision Productions Inc, Founder, Published Author

"Gio is a leader in the community. His dedication to personal growth and development is encouraging, and his determination to succeed is what has inspired me the most."

- Raul Marin, Sr. Mgr. of Online Learning at LCMC

"Since the moment I met Gio, he has kept a positive attitude. His passion for helping others reach their full potential is amazing. Giovanni is an example of what dedication and passion looks like."

- Carmen Gonzalez, CEO of Writing Moves Me

"Gio Is An Amazing Young Man! He Automatically Draws Your Attention Because of His Sincerity & Passion To Help Others. Gio Definitely Encouraged Me & Inspired Me When I Heard Him Speak At A Corporate Event. Keep Up The Great Work Gio! YurrrP!!!"

- DJ MILK D/CEO of BOURGEOIS ENT. LLC/YurrrP Radio

"Gio is by far the youngest, most inspiring person I know. He is a role model for all the upcoming generations."

- Gaby Abdelgadir, Certified Canfield Success Principles Trainer

"My son did not have an easy life growing up and his perseverance, discipline, and strength continues to blow me away. Giovanni continued to show the world his love, despite facing poverty and poor overall health. Giovanni is a hero to a lot of people and I am so proud of my baby boy."

- Olga E. Garcia-Negron, Mother of Giovanni Negron-Garcia

"Raising Giovanni was no easy task, but I am proud of the man he has become. His discipline is unmatched, and he is not scared to sacrifice everything he has for others to see glory. My son continues to make our family proud, and I am happy to still be here to witness the inspiration my son has become around the world"

- Joel I. Negron-Colon, Father of Giovanni Negron-Garcia

"My brother continues to show the world that he will not be denied of his dream. I have never seen someone so committed to helping others succeed after going down a rough patch himself. Giovanni continues to "Go. Inspire. Others."

- Joel I. Negron-Garcia, Brother of Giovanni Negron-Garcia

"My brother continues make a positive impact! His dedication and passion towards helping people find their glory is astonishing. I am so proud of my baby brother, and he is only going up from here."

- Joelienid Negron-Garcia, Sister of Giovanni Negron-Garcia

"Gio is a man of passion, resilience and determination. He immediately impacted my life from the first day I met him with inspiration and wisdom beyond his years. I'm grateful and honored to know him."

- Jose Escobar, CEO & Founder of The Entrepreneur's Bookshelf

"Gio opened my eyes during his keynote showing me that anything in life is possible, and that you can overcome all your challenges no matter how big or scary they seem. I was inspired listening to him speak as he commanded the stage. In addition, he's also a super nice guy and I enjoyed our conversation following his keynote."

- Bruce Serbin - CEO of Serbin Media, Inc.

Preface

Passion, Purpose, and the Pursuit of Happiness is written for individuals looking to define who they are and why they are pursuing the career of their dreams. Defining our passion and purpose is a critical stage in our lives. It establishes direction and reason during our journey. Without these tools, life can be misleading and miserable. Life is not intended to be lived without love and happiness. We are all in different stages of our lives, and how we define passion and purpose varies from person to person. We should never seek to compare or compete with other individuals because we are blessed with unique gifts. The gifts we are blessed with are specially crafted for us to embrace and use. Wanting the gifts of someone else will take us off course and lead us down a path that was not designed for us to walk on.

After you are done reading this book, fuel will be added to your fire! A clear definition of your passion and purpose will come to light, and action can be taken towards your aspirations. Please use this book as a tool during the construction of your dream-building process. Remember that our passion and purpose can change at any time, and it is nothing to stress about. Life can change at any given moment, and you will have to come up with a plan to adapt to those changes. While reading this book, your goal is to reflect after reading each chapter. Take some time to think about what you just read and write out some action steps on how to grow your passion and establish your purpose. You do not necessarily need a clear definition of your passion and purpose when reading this book. But, if you already have a strong sense of passion and purpose, congratulations! Use this book as a tool to refine and strengthen your passion and purpose. Re-read the chapters if you must. There should be no rush to finishing it.

Developing passion and purpose is a process. Try to rush it and you will find yourself stuck and confused.

There is an important component that some people overlook while searching for their passion and purpose; and that is their pursuit of happiness. Happiness should be at the center of everything you do. I can bet you $100 that you know at least one person who is not happy and complains about it daily. If this happens to be you, then purchasing this book was the right move. Happiness is not measured by the amount of money or luxuries that you possess. Happiness is something you feel and brings the best out of you. There are people with an abundance of wealth who are also some of the saddest people you will ever meet. Happiness is achieved through accomplishments and knowing we are fully fulfilling our potential. When you reach the chapters about happiness, ask yourself this question, "Am I truly happy?" If the answer is "no", that is perfectly fine. If the answer is "yes", awesome! If you are unsure, that is also perfectly fine! The pursuit of happiness is a process, and it will be addressed in this book.

The journey starts now! Good luck and do not hesitate to stop if you are becoming overwhelmed during any point in this process. Remember to breath, remain hydrated, and reflect whenever possible. This process has no timeline and can be done at any stage of life. Finding your passion and purpose is no easy task. The fact that you are taking this challenge head on is a huge achievement and you should be proud of yourself for it! Fight for your dreams and keep them alive at all costs. There will be times when you will want to quit. There will be people who will try to belittle your growth. Whatever you do, never stop fighting for your dreams! Claim your glory and fall in love with your process. Make yourself a believer and serve as an inspiration to those who need a role model. Thank you for taking the time to better yourself and your future. I am so proud of you. Use this book as a guide and a tool towards your growth. Now go out and find your passion, purpose, and pursuit of happiness!

Chapter 1

What is Passion?

Welcome to the first step of your journey, and that is defining your passion. What comes to mind when you hear the word passion? Some think of passion in the sense of romance or a barely controllable emotion. When talking about passion in this book, passion means the oxygen for the soul. Passion is the fuel to your fire. This is why, when a boy scout starts a fire, he needs to blow on the spark to spread the fire. The same way a human needs oxygen to stay alive and well.

Keeping your passion alive will be tough. Some people are going to try to extinguish your fire because it burns brighter than their own. Sometimes, we put our attention somewhere else, and the fire eventually dies out because we did not attend to it in time. Some people may even use your fire because they are incapable of igniting their own. Letting other people use your fire is a good thing only if they agree to help you keep it burning. When we let others use our fire, we are allowing them to use our energy. If our energy is not restored, our fire will slowly lose its flame. If we are not maintaining the fire within us, our dreams and aspirations will die. Our dreams and aspirations live off our passion, which is the oxygen to our fire. Get it now? Great! Please do not make me draw it out for you, I suck at drawing.

Maintaining your passion takes practice and understanding. For example, I always had the dream of being a public speaker. I was excited for every opportunity I had to speak in front of people, no matter the occasion. There was a time when I was invited to be a speaker at an annual Hispanic Heritage Gala. I was only 17 and still in high school, at the time, but I was so excited to have my chance to speak in front of some important people. I told my peers and family about it, and they were all excited for me. However, a classmate of mine heard about my opportunity and for some apparent reason yelled out, "Gio, no one honestly cares about what you have to say. Public speaking is stupid, and they are not going to care. I promise you that." My teacher asked my classmate to leave the classroom and go straight to the principal's office. I never understood why they said that, but my only assumption was they did not like me. At the time of the incident, that comment was a huge blow to my confidence. The question that swarmed my head was, 'Does nobody care about my public speaking dream?' I went home and practiced my speech for hours. I kept on mispronouncing words, missing ques, and going over the time I was given to speak. I truly felt defeated and realized that being a public speaker was not really a dream to pursue. My mother came into my room and saw me in distraught. She looked me and said, "Why do you look sad baby boy? Your speech sounded amazing my love." I was confused by her comment and ranted about screwing up so many times during my practice runs. I even told her about what happened at school with my classmate. She took a seat next to me on my bed and said, "Gio, we are all going to screw up sometimes in life and there will be people there to never let you forget about it. What you do is keep on trying and never let anyone interfere with your dream. That belongs to you, and you need to own it." This made me feel great and I kept on practicing.

The day of the Gala came, and I delivered my speech. I noticed a lot of people on their phones and continuing their side conversations. They did not care about the high school kid on the stage for they did not expect much from him. However, that did not stop me from delivering the speech that earned me a standing ovation in the end. The speech was about not quitting on our dreams, even though we are living in poverty and seeing our community members being affected by the city's drug epidemic, crime rate, and constant gun shootings. That standing ovation fueled my fire of becoming a public speaker, and now I own my life coaching and public speaking company.

I shared this story with you because of the fact that we are responsible for whether or not we allow our passions to die. There will be life events and people that will test your passion; and how we decide to react to it is going to determine whether we are going to fulfill our dreams and aspirations. I could have easily believed what was said by my classmate and stopped speaking entirely. But I decided to listen to my mother instead and believe in the voice with which I was blessed to create an impact within my own community.

Remember that the only person who will be able to see the bigger picture is the artist holding the paint brush. We must understand that having passion is a gift that many want but only a special few can harness its true power. Having passion will allow you to unlock potential that you were not aware of before. Passion is the oxygen of the soul and the reason why some of us wake up before the nine alarms we set on our phone to get up in the morning (trust me, I have seen people with more than twenty). Establishing passion during your journey can help zone out those negative voices and external forces that are preventing you from reaching your potential. Do not just define your passion, claim it!

One important lesson to learn with passion is to never let money influence it. Yes, money is essential to everyday living, but it should not be your primary driving force. What if the money you expected to make does not come? Does your passion die? Was every accomplishment a complete waste of time? Please reflect on these questions when developing your passion. Money does provide the essentials, but it does not measure the value of self-worth or personal achievements. Developing a strong sense of passion will make you feel like a billionaire without even having the funds! Some of the wealthiest people in the world have no clear definition of what their passion is other than making money. If they lost the money they possess now, they would have nothing and would most likely be called a failure by society.

Having passion can improve the quality of your life. Passion can take you from your darkest moments and drive you into some of the best days that you have ever lived. Passion serves as the driving force to make change and understand why we should live out our vision. If I didn't find my passion, I would be dead right now (this is not an exaggeration). I was once 366 pounds with moderate sleep apnea and other health complications that put a strain on my life expectancy. I lost my drive to do anything in life. I was in my junior year of college and only twenty-one years old. And, in September of 2018, I found out that I was cheated on. At that time, I felt that my love no longer had value. This is where I recognized I was replaceable and worthless to someone who claimed they loved me. My ex-girlfriend treated me as if I was some old toy that she got tired of using. I felt I had failed as a man and lost the one thing I promised to protect. What hurt the most was that I had planned to propose to her that Christmas, but that dream turned into my worst nightmare. I lost my sense of pride and isolated myself from family and friends. Opportunities were flying over my head, and I did nothing to push myself. I had no money and spent the winter of 2018 in my college apartment with no electricity and barely any food.

I was facing the toughest time of my life and my health was not making it any better. It got to the point where I was being publicly humiliated and shunned by people I believed to be my friends. I will never forget the time when I left the dining hall of my university and a woman who lived in the suite style dorm opened her window and said, "You are so fat, you should kill yourself!" Considering what I was feeling at that point, I did not disagree with her. I was miserable and did not believe my life could get any worse. I felt like my final days were ahead of me and I had no reason to fight anymore.

That was until my yearly check-up when I found out that things really could come to an end early for me. My physician looked me right in the eye and said, "Giovanni, do not plan to have any dreams and aspirations past 35 because the way you are going, I do not believe you are going to see those days." At that very moment, it became clear to me that I needed to reignite the fire that was within me. It was clear, I needed to sum up all the courage, strength, and faith I had left and fight for my life! There was no way that I could not live past thirty-five. I must witness my brother get married to his girlfriend. I must be there when my mother is retired and can live peacefully with my father in their home of Puerto Rico. I must provide my sister first class travel to wherever she wants to explore. Some people believed in me, and I could not let them down. I wanted to be a father and be there for my wife. I had a vision of headlining conferences all over the world and inspiring over 10 million people in my lifetime through my speaking engagements. My family did not deserve to see me die young and live with guilt the rest of their lives. My supporters will become disappointed and believe my message of passion and purpose was just a lie. Thirty-five was way too soon to see the end and I refused to die without participating in the fight of my life!

So, I stepped up to the challenge! I removed all the excuses and negativity from my life and replaced them with positive affirmation and progressive action. I invested in my health by getting bariatric sleeve surgery. I put all my anger and sorrow into my workouts. I groomed my heart, my mind, and my soul so that it reflected my vision. Everything changed! My eating habits, my behaviors, my drive, and even my passion. My passion grew every day to revive my dream of being a life coach and support all those who are going through a life-changing journey of their own. The fire within was growing and all the doubt within was fading away. I wanted to claim all the glory that was lost. The vision of living a healthier and energetic life kept my passion alive. My fire was burning so bright that I transformed my body, mind, and soul in the span of year. I once weighed 366 pounds but now had lost over 180 pounds. I reached my goal weight of 180 pounds and went back to see the same physician. Looked him right in the eye and said, "Thirty-five was not enough time. I plan on needing more if that is okay with you."

My passion for life and wanting more out of it led me to find out who I was and what I can do. Passion is powerful and it is life-changing. Passion can be achieved through discipline and consistency with your vision. Do not believe that the circumstances you are facing right now are preventing you from fulfilling your vision. What is preventing you is what lies between your ears and shoulders. The battle we have with ourselves is going to be the hardest battle we will ever fight in our lives. We must change our mindsets to implement change in our lives. Let passion become your guide. Allow your passion to be your energy source and do not let anyone drain you of that energy. Passion is already instilled in you and all you must do is find it through reflection and action. Passion is a tool in life that you do not want to live without. Protect your passion and let it guide you to the glory that you have not claimed yet. Now let us move on to the next part of passion and that is the question, "Can we become too passionate about something?"

Reflect:

What are you passionate about? Why does it matter to you?

How will your passion benefit your dream?

Chapter 2:

"Am I Too Passionate?"

As mentioned in chapter one, passion can be defined as a strong or barely controllable emotion. Our passion can grow so much that it can become infectious and rub off onto the people that surround us. Those who appreciate your passion will acknowledge you and benefit from it. Those who do not appreciate it will cringe at your presence. At times, they will say, "They are doing too much;" or "They are too full of themselves." Those people are either jealous or cannot stand the fact that we figured out a way to remain passionate despite personal setbacks. Once momentum is gained during your journey, the fire within keeps on burning brighter. That warm feeling inside of you brings comfort and excitement! But sometimes that fire can spread into areas where it is not wanted or needed. For example, you may be passionate about the development of undergraduate college students, but your colleagues do not share that same passion and express that they do not want you to outshine them. When this happens, it usually has some backlash and can stop the momentum that was gained. The question then creeps into your head, "Am I too passionate?"

The answer to that question is no. Nobody is ever too passionate about something. We can never stop being passionate about the things we love to do. We can agree to disagree on this topic but think about how many people are passionate today vs. those who are struggling to find what they are passionate about. The point I am trying to make here is that we must use our passion where it is needed and welcomed. We do not want our fire spreading into areas where it can be extinguished. Maintaining our passion requires discipline and focus. Passionate individuals are some of the most energetic people we will ever meet in our lifetime. Energy can be drained easily by individuals who do not appreciate it or by those who have their own personal agenda. We must be careful where we carry our passion.

My momentum was at an all-time high after performing my speech during the Hispanic Heritage Gala in 2017. Influential community leaders came up to me and informed me of how well I did. Some were really impressed by the speech and others missed the speech entirely because they were on their phones. I started building my network that night and a gentleman walked up to me to tell me about an opportunity to join their campaign team. They told me I could be their spokesperson and that my "young" voice is important to their campaign. At that time, I did not realize what was going on, but I agreed to do it because I believed I was doing something beneficial towards my passion. Turns out it was just an attempt to show investors and eligible voters that the candidate "supports the young people". They had their own agenda of winning the election and knew the way to win was to take aim at the one thing my hometown takes great pride in - our youth. For the sake of my peace, I will not reveal this person's name. Just know they were elected to local office in Reading, PA and forgot I ever existed after winning.

My confidence and momentum took a major hit from this experience. I believed that someone took interest in my passion of public speaking and creating change. Turns out they only used me for money, votes, and a seat at the table. I share this story to show that carrying your passion into areas that are not needed can have a lasting effect on your growth. The self-doubt grew to the point I almost quit speaking entirely and never wanted to promote positive change ever again. Being forgotten is something that no one deserves to experience in their lifetime.

Display your passion in areas where it is appreciated and welcomed. Before allowing anyone to use your energy for their efforts, do not be afraid to ask what their intentions are and how your passion relates to their project. Remember, energy is an investment, and no one should ever think you owe them your energy because they are doing something you are passionate about. Unfortunately, some people will take advantage of that just so they can receive the credit and their seat at the table. They will take your investment and forget that you even exist. But I know you exist. I acknowledge you and I want to say that I am proud of you. You are doing a great job. Whoever tells you otherwise, screw them! You are enough and nobody should ever make you feel less. Got it? Good!

Protecting our passion is critical when it comes to our growth and development. Since it is a barely controllable emotion, we do not want to become full of ourselves. We must remain humble and value the gift with which we are blessed. Being passionate can often be confused with being conceited because it displays a level of confidence and self-love that only we learn to appreciate overtime. Passionate people are not afraid to show it because they want other people to know the gift that was claimed. We can easily get caught up in ourselves without noticing it and this will send a bad impression to the people who support you. Therefore, reflection is important during our passion development process. Reflecting on our actions and how we display our passion can provide better insight on how someone may perceive us and what we could do to not seem self-centered. Now, it is completely necessary to be selfish at times because we must keep our momentum going. We must make sure that we are okay and that the fire within us is still burning bright. What we do not want is to drive people away because we think we have all the answers, and our passion makes us better than those who surround us.

    I was in the middle of completing my senior year at Kutztown University of Pennsylvania and my confidence was through the roof. I was finding great success with my weight loss journey and, through helping my peers overcome their personal hardships, my passion kept on growing. I was so ahead in my studies that I already knew I was graduating and all they needed to do was to send me my degree (I literally had nothing to do academically for two months). With all the excitement and energy brewing inside of me, I thought it would be time for me to get back in the dating scene.

There was a beautiful Afro-Latina woman that I've been crushing on since my sophomore year of college. She has beautiful curly hair, caramel complexion, and a fantastic personality. I knew she was single, and I finally collected enough courage to ask her out on a date. To my surprise, she said yes! I arrived at the restaurant early so that I could pull out her chair when she takes a seat. The time in which we both agreed to meet up was already approaching and she had not arrived. Half an hour went by, and she still had not arrived. My waiter had asked 2 times if

I wanted to order anything and I kept on saying, "I am waiting for someone." No text, no phone call, and I have been waiting in the restaurant for two hours already. I was embarrassed and I believe the waiter caught on to what happened. The waiter came over and said, "I am sorry for what happened to you. Your meal is on us tonight." I went home devastated and could not believe I was stood up like that. The next day, I saw the woman and asked why she did not show up to our date. She said, "Gio, I'm so sorry about last night, but I cannot date someone who is about themselves." At that moment, I almost exploded because I had done so much more for other people than focus on my health. But I let her continue.

Although I still found it rude that I was stood up, I understood what she was saying. It had nothing to do with who I was, but it had everything to do with my character. You are probably reading this and saying, "But Gio! She made you wait two hours in a restaurant and that is messed up!" That is true, but it made me reflect on how I was displaying myself after losing weight and reclaiming my passion. I must admit that I was gloating more than I was celebrating. I wanted people to acknowledge me, and I went on long rants about myself. Although it was an inspiring journey, I could have let my actions and results do the talking for me. This is where I learned the importance of being humble and knowing that it is okay if not everyone knows what I am about. If I had controlled my passion and had just been me, I would probably still be seeing this person. When establishing your passion, it is not a bad idea to do a self-check and ask your peers if you are coming off as conceited. The truth may hurt, but it is only to make you better.

As I addressed earlier in this chapter, we are never too passionate about what we love to do. Yes, there are things we can work on to ensure our passion does not rub someone the wrong way, but it is perfectly fine to remain passionate. Have you ever been told that you are too passionate? Reflect on how that made you feel for a moment. Usually when this question arises, it stops our momentum because we are worried we are moving too fast. Sometimes we start to think that we are annoying other people with our progress. The need for validation starts to kick in and that is when things become complicated. Wanting validation during this stage of your journey is what I like to call a "dream killer".

If you did not know before, validation is the recognition or affirmation of either a person or their feelings or opinions. We seek validation to ensure that we have support, and it even serves as the green light for us to continue moving forward with our dreams. The reason I call validation a "dream killer" is because, the moment it is not received, it kills any progress that was made and can make certain individuals lose their passion immediately. You are probably reading this and saying to yourself, "How is that even possible?! Who cares about what other people think?" As humans, we want to be loved, accepted, and supported by other people. We want to know that whatever we are doing, our supporters are going to be there and cheer us on. We believe our mentors will be there to guide us and that we will receive their approval without any conflict. When these things are not present, it creates doubt, and the individual begins to worry about whether their dream is even worth pursuing. It is important that we do not become too dependent on validation and can make choices that we know will be best for us.

This reminds me of the time I started to think about applying to graduate school. I planned on earning my master's degree in Student Affairs in Higher Education. My goal was to earn a career as an admissions counselor at an undergraduate institution. I submitted my application to Indiana University of Pennsylvania and was accepted two months after applying. I was so proud of myself and excited for what was to come! I shared the news with family, peers, colleagues, and my mentors. I expected to receive approval from them all since it was a huge milestone for me, but I received a mixed reaction that created doubt within me. My family told me they were proud, and they were supportive of my decision to go to graduate school. However, some of my peers believed I was wasting my time and money. They even went as far as to tell me that college is a scam and that our degrees are worthless. A curveball was thrown at me when one of my colleagues questioned my work ethic and was not sure if going to graduate school was a smart move (this person was just miserable). My mentors asked if I was sure about going to graduate school, which is what a good mentor would do. But this caused me to reflect on my decision about going to graduate school because now I was not sure if I was ready for it.

During my reflection, I was starting to believe that graduate school was not for me. Then I asked myself, "Why are you asking people about their opinions when you made the decision to apply on your own?" I realized that this was not for them, earning my master's degree was for me and my legacy. I informed everyone that I would be continuing my education at IUP after I graduate from Kutztown University. Those who did not agree with my decision would just have to live with it. Those who supported me were proud and excited for the journey I was going to embark on. I am currently earning my master's degree in student affairs right now. It is awesome and I am so happy that I made the decision to go for it!

I share this story to let you know that we must make decisions for ourselves and not be too dependent on other people's opinions. We know better than anyone else what is best for us and what will lead us to our dreams. People will share their opinions based on their experiences and what they believe is right for you. Hear them out, but do not let it have a major influence in your final decision. Your passion is the thing at risk here and you should only make decisions that will keep your fire burning bright. Therefore, I say, you can never be too passionate about something. Those people from whom we seek validation may not be passionate themselves and can be the reason our dreams die. Being passionate about goals and dreams can help guide us to independence and glory. When the passion grows within you, we must harness its power and never let go. Whatever you desire to be passionate about, claim it and never be afraid to let people know what you are passionate about. If I allowed other people to influence my choices, I would probably be miserable and in the same condition that I was in before. Understand that developing your passion requires great discipline and patience. Having passion is a true blessing, but it would not live up to its full potential if you did not understand the reason behind it.

Now, it is time to dig even deeper into your journey and find your "why?".

Reflect:

Was there ever a time in which you were told that you were too passionate about something? How did that make you feel? Did it stop your momentum? How did you approach this situation? What can you do now to ensure it does not happen again?

Chapter 3:

What is Purpose?

When progressing through your journey, it is important to understand why we are doing certain things to promote our growth and passion. Purpose is the reason for which something is done or created or for which something exists. With no purpose there will be no reason behind any of our actions and goals. Everything we do will just seem pointless and will eventually burn out the fire we have within. Have you ever been asked why you did something and had absolutely no clue as to why you did it? Don't worry, it is okay to say yes; most of us did as well. This is because we tend to do things based off our passion alone and rarely ask ourselves why we are passionate about doing the things we do.

I was booked for a speaking engagement at Penn State Berks in 2019. My passion for public speaking grew immensely and I loved sharing my story of overcoming hardships with other people, especially college students. The atmosphere was amazing! Students were engaged, I was not screwing up my lines, and the faculty in attendance were enjoying themselves as well. The speaking engagement was nearing its end and I usually save the last 15 minutes for a Q/A session. Normally, I don't get any questions during this time because the student is too shy to ask his or her question in front of the group. This particular time, a first-year student raised their hand and asked me a question that threw me off. Their question was, "Why do you perform motivational speeches?" You would think I would have a clear and concise answer to this question, but I did not. I thought quickly and said, "I just love speaking and helping others achieve their dreams." The student nodded their head, but I knew at that moment I had no idea why I continued doing speaking engagements. I just knew that I loved doing it and it provided a chance to share my gift with those who need to find direction in their lives. I got home that night and immediately went to my room for a reflection session. During this time, I realized that my passion would not be sufficient to carry on my dream. My dream needed reason to it, and I needed to find purpose.

Finding purpose is not as easy as you may think. See, we know what makes us passionate about certain things, but we never think deeper and wonder why we are passionate about these certain things. Finding your purpose requires reflection and understanding. I've developed three questions that will help you better define your purpose: (1) Why am I doing this? (2) Does this reflect who I am? (3) Is this something that I am proud of? Allow me to break down each question for you, so when you decide to develop your purpose statement, it will be a smooth process. Remember that, when you develop your purpose statement, it may change overtime and that is perfectly fine. The important lesson to learn here is that we need to have reason to support our passion.

Why am I Doing This?

If you cannot answer this question, then maybe it is time to reconsider what you are doing. Please do not think what you are currently doing is not enough, but it is important to consider that we should have an established reason as to why we do certain things related to our passion. This question is the toughest question out of the three to answer because it puts things into perspective. We, sometimes, do not check-in with ourselves and, instead, do things based on passion alone which makes things unclear to some people and they begin to question your intentions and authenticity.

For example, let's say that you organized a fundraiser that will benefit community centers that serve underprivileged teens. You are aware that philanthropy is one of your passions and will not turn down an opportunity to help the youth. A local news station wants to interview you and a reporter asks, "Why did you organize this fundraiser?" Some of us would automatically answer, "I did this for our youth." This is a great answer, but it does not answer why numerous hours of planning went into creating this event. Anyone can say this, and no work was put on their end to make the fundraiser possible. An answer you may want to consider is, "The reason I put this fundraiser together is to help underprivileged teens receive the support they need so that they can pursue their dreams and goals." It is a longer answer, but now people understand the real reason why you are passionate about this project. It has purpose behind.

Understanding why you are doing something is important when building your character. Not understanding the reason why something is being done on your end can seem inauthentic. People will start to question whether you are passionate or only doing certain things to gain approval. So, next time you are asked the question, "Why are you doing this?"; take a moment to think and make sure to put a reason behind your actions. This will provide clarity and understanding, and it will also allow you to maintain your authentic character. Finding your "why" takes some time; so please do not feel there is a timeline to find it. I know people who are in their 50s and still working on finding their "why". I have been asked numerous times about my reason behind certain initiatives, and I could not provide a clear answer. Some people even questioned my authenticity because they felt I had no reason behind anything I did. They felt I only did things for the recognition and that was far from the truth. To avoid these challenges, think about these things before acting and let the world know that you are doing what you are doing with reason!

Does This Reflect Who I am?

We must be cautious as to with whom and what we involve ourselves. Sometimes we get caught up with certain people or events that make us feel good now but can create a situation where we don't recognize the person we see in the mirror. There is nothing wrong with being put in this situation because it does happen to the best of us. The severity of the situation varies from person to person and the three things we must do to get back on track is: (1) refocus, (2) reflect, and (3) find forgiveness.

We often get caught up in the moment and put our needs first, then insert our logical thinking. Again, we are human and there is no need to be harsh on yourself when things take a bad turn. When developing your purpose statement, it is important to also develop a strong sense of self. Developing a strong sense of self establishes awareness of self-value and importance. When we have great understanding of who we are, we become more aware of the situations we should avoid so that we do not affect our momentum. Please take note that when we know our worth in this world, there is no negotiating it with someone else. When we move up in life and things are going great, we cannot lose our sense of self.

At one point of my life, I felt like I was unstoppable. I had the most beautiful girlfriend, I was finally recognized as a community leader, and I had earned the title of being role model for young professionals. These things fed into my ego and took my attention away from my passion and purpose. I took a picture to post on social media and it was weird to say that I did not recognize the person in the photo. On that day, something was off, and I felt something bad was going to happen to me. I refused to leave my college dorm that day because I believed I was going to experience a pain from which I would not recover. It was fall and the day was gorgeous, but I spent the entire day in my room and only left for food. Long story short, my girlfriend at the time admitted to having an affair while I was attending college and this killed all the momentum I had (if you are reading this, I forgive you and love you).

During this stage of my life, I was doing things that did not reflect who I was and what I stood for, but the pain was too much for me to handle and I needed to find a way to cope. Food, social media, pointless sexual encounters, and constant need for validation was what I engaged in, which led me to losing my sense of self. This downward spiral almost put me out for the count and only a miracle could save me. This also contributed to health complications that I mentioned earlier in this book. For me to make a comeback from this terrible situation, I needed to do three things: (1) refocus, (2) reflect, and (3) find forgiveness. It took me four years to recover, but the lesson to learn here is that we must find ourselves again to move forward. When pursuing certain things in our lives, we must stop and ask, "Does this reflect who I am?", so we do not forget who we are and why we are still progressing towards our dreams and aspirations.

Is This Something I am Proud of?

Growing up in a Puerto Rican household, maintaining our pride and discipline was an important value to my family. My parents did an excellent job of reassuring their children of how proud they were and that we should also be proud of what we accomplished. We must be proud of ourselves because we cannot base our success on how proud other people are of us. Yes, it is great to know that other people are proud of you, but it should not be the primary reason why you are chasing after your goals and aspirations. My parents will always be proud of me, but I am not going after my dreams for that reason. I love and admire them, but they are not creating the progress for my journey, that is solely on me. We must make ourselves believers in our purpose before anyone else. If you are not proud of what you do, then you either need to evaluate what is going on or realize that you are not doing the thing you are gifted at.

Being proud of yourself can often be mistaken as gloating. Unfortunately, we encounter some individuals that cannot live with the fact that some of us take great pride in our successes (these people are the absolute worse). Never be afraid to claim your glory! Just remember to remain humble and do not shove it down someone's throat. There is absolutely nothing wrong with being proud of yourself. If I am being honest, it is necessary when developing your purpose because it establishes more confidence in your passion. Again, not being proud of what you do can make you seem inauthentic and not interested in what you should be passionate about.

When I earned my full-tuition scholarship to Kutztown University of Pennsylvania, I was so proud of myself. I told everyone about it! I told my family members, my peers, the school janitor, the lunch lady, the homeless guy by my favorite corner store, and I think you get the point. Getting this scholarship created opportunities for me that I believed would allow me to fulfill my passion and purpose. Of course, I encountered some individuals who thought I was not deserving of the scholarship because I did not take AP classes in high school (please do not let this discourage you from taking AP courses. Take them and earn college credits before even attending college). What I did was internalize my reason for wanting to go to college and ignored the "haters". Developing your purpose is a challenge but imagine the power that will be possessed once you internalize your purpose and are committed to changes that are going to come during the progression of your journey.

Reflect:

What is your purpose? Why are you doing what you are doing? Does it make you happy? Does it reflect who you are? Is it something you are proud of?

Chapter 4:

Internalizing Your Purpose

Now that there is reason behind your passion, the next part is accepting your "why" and allowing it to be your guide. Accepting your purpose is a huge commitment because change is going to come and some of us may not be ready for that. Your purpose will guide you away from people who do not support and understand your vision, which can include family members, peers, and colleagues. Your purpose will also guide you into new areas that will force you out of your comfort zone. Leaving your comfort zone will promote growth and adaptability, which will reduce anxiety and discomfort when encountering new experiences. Purpose serves as the progressive guide for our passion, and it will not stop providing reason as to why our potential cannot reach its fullest extent.

I know this is a lot to take in, so please take deep breath, take of sip of water, and know that internalizing your purpose is a process with no timeline. Do not feel rushed to internalize your purpose because it is best to take some time and process the changes that are going to occur. We must form a relationship with our "guide" so that boundaries are established, and a commitment is made for a long-term relationship. Yes, you are going to encounter some challenges and even may experience some lonely days, but your purpose will guide you through the tough times and ensure you come out on top!

During the winter of 2018, I did not have a single dollar to my name. I was forced to shut off my electricity in my college apartment and depend on Kutztown University's food bank to feed myself (there is no shame in this, we must do whatever is necessary to survive). No pun intended; I was facing the darkest days of my young life. The nights were long, lonely, miserable, and cold. I questioned how my purpose could lead me to such a low point in my journey. I will never forget the night when I raised my fist to the ceiling in anger and yelled, "I was the one who was cheated on! Death is on my heels, and now my own purpose wants to betray me!" I eventually fell asleep from exhaustion and depression kicking my butt. It was about two in the morning, and something woke me up. A burning sensation flowed through my body and an abundance of energy started to flow through my veins. It was late in the night to reflect, but I realized why this was all happening. It was because change was coming, and I needed to relive my days of poverty so that I can understand good days will always arrive to those who remain patient. I needed to understand and experience what the lowest point of my life is going to look like if I did not take control of my life.

Our purpose in life will always guide us to understanding and acceptance. We will encounter situations where we will feel hopeless and, during that time, feel that we are forced to settle for less. What your internalized purpose will do in this situation is become your progressive guide and reignite the fire that is within you. We become aware that we must groom our minds and hearts for us to claim the glory we crave. Purpose is the greatest tool to possess, and it will be the most useful when encountering hardships. There is a reason behind everything that happens in our lives, but it is our choice if we choose to accept the circumstances or create the change that will benefit our growth and development.

The first step to internalizing your purpose is writing it down on a piece of paper and repeating it to yourself five times in front of a mirror every day. This may seem excessive, but we can easily forget our purpose once confronted with an issue or a sudden change. Completing this step will engrain your purpose into your mindset and you will become more aware of your purpose as your journey progresses. While you are at it, add some words of positive affirmation. These are words that provide you with emotional support and encouragement. Internalizing your purpose requires us to be in the right mindset; and reminding ourselves of how unique we are can make the process smoother.

The second step to internalizing your purpose is being consistent with your action plan. Lack of consistency can cause disappointment because results are not being produced. What can be done to avoid this is setting up an action plan. What you do is write your short-term or long-term goals on a piece of paper and make it as specific as possible. With this goal, you must make sure it is attainable within the timeframe that is set. For example, my long-term goal is to publish 2 books by October 25th, 2022. This goal is specific, measurable, attainable, realistic, and time bound. If your goal is established, then you can move on and create the action steps necessary to achieve your goal.

For example, publishing 2 books by October 25th, 2022, will require me to: (1) type at least 500 words a day, (2) put together a focus group to help me develop a book cover, (3) find beta readers to provide feedback, (4) create a book title, and (5) find a publisher. From a financial goal perspective, I would suggest saving at least $2,500 to $3,000. Saving up this money will help you hire an editor, secure your copyright and ISBN number, and as well secure services that will help you market and sell your book. Take some time to reflect on what your short-term and long-term goal is, then create an action plan based on the examples that were provided. This will help you remain consistent with achieving your goals.

The last step to internalizing your purpose is taking ownership of it. The reason this is the last step is because you want to test it out before committing to it. We must believe in our purpose to fulfill its potential. If you develop a sense of purpose that does not reflect your passion, then your actions will be meaningless and will be done on passion alone. Taking ownership of your purpose also means not comparing it to another person's purpose. Your purpose was specially crafted for you and there is no need to make it a competition with someone else. If you do, then chances are you will become miserable because you want something of someone that does not belong to you. Some people fail to reach their goals because of not being grateful for what they established for themselves and, instead, went after the gifts of other people. Do not allow yourself to get to this point and ruin all the progress that was made. As I mentioned before, your purpose can be changed so that it can match the current situation you are in. That is why your purpose is your guide because it will always lead you to where you need to be!

Completing these 3 steps will not only help you internalize your purpose, but it will also help you remain committed to your journey. Quitting should not be an option just because you cannot see the light at the end of the tunnel and feel you don't have the strength to continue. We must condition ourselves to know how to react to our wins and losses. Developing your passion and purpose is not always sunshine and rainbows. This journey you embark on is going to humble you, so please do not have the expectation that your journey is going to be smooth sailing if everything is done right. We must experience hardship to see how far we are willing to go for our passion and purpose. I am not saying to go broke and go an entire winter without electricity and food but rather to have the expectation that hardships will occur and how you react will determine what you are willing to fight for.

Commitment is something that some of us are not fans of. When we think of commitment, we think about the amount of effort we are putting into something and sticking with it until the job is done. The reason some of us are not fans of commitment is due to the amount work, time, and effort that goes into achieving our dreams and long-term goals. Walt Disney once said, "If you can dream it, you can do it," and some would argue that this is a false reality because not everyone achieves their dream. Thinking and talking about your dream is the easy part but taking the first step to pursue it is the hardest task of the entire process. Achieving your dreams should not be a false reality, especially when we spend most of our lives asking ourselves, "What if?", instead of taking action and creating progress towards our dreams.

Committing to your passion and purpose should not be a negotiation. We should never negotiate when it comes to our dreams. Yes, we can adjust our purpose to create progress in our journey, but we cannot expect the same when it comes to our dreams. Not committing to your dreams is the same as quitting on yourself. You already established a reason why you are pursuing your dream and now you must just go for it! The fear of pursuing our dreams is created by the doubt we have about our futures and not wanting to leave our comfort zone. We must make sacrifices to see our dreams come true. What you don't want to happen is to be in your 70s arguing with yourself as to why you did not take the chance to pursue your dreams.

When I began my career as a public speaker, I was only 15 years old. If I am being honest, I was not any good in the beginning of my career. I had no clear message and the only reason I started speaking was because of my passion for helping people. I would spend hours after school asking my teachers if they would allow me to speak during their classes and they told me no. I would ask local community members if they would give me some time to speak during public events and they told me no. As mentioned earlier in this book, I was even told that my voice does not matter, and no one would care for what I had to say. As a public speaker, my main goal is to headline a sold-out Madison Square Garden. It is a shame that the people of my hometown of Reading, PA were not supportive of my dream and would tease me every time I brought it up. I stopped speaking after I graduated high school and believed my dream was stupid after being told no so many times.

Obviously, that is not the case now because I own Gio Effect Life Coaching and Public Speaking, LLC. I returned to speaking because I recognized that I love what I do. The reason I do it now is to help underprivileged professionals achieve their goals and dreams based on their career aspirations. I did not want to grow up old and argue with myself as to why I did not pursue my dream of being a well-known public speaker. You should not have to, either. Once the dream is already created in your head, it belongs to you, and it is your responsibility to bring it to life. Who cares if your dream is not popular to other people and that it is going to take years to come true? I would hate to wake up another day not doing something for which I am gifted. I would hate to die knowing that I had the chance to make something great out of my gift and I chose not to because I feared failing. Internalize your purpose and allow it to lead you where you need to go. Do not quit on your dreams because you don't want to fail. A lot of us failed multiple times before we could live in our gift. You have the potential to achieve anything you set your mind to and now all you must do is believe. Now that you found reason behind your passion, let me ask you a question, "Do you believe happiness should be the center of everything we do?"

Reflect:

How will you internalize your purpose? Are you willing to commit to your purpose? What steps need to be taken to ensure your purpose lives up to its full potential?

Chapter 5:

The Pursuit of Happiness

The one thing I feel that all people share is their craving for happiness. Happiness can be defined as a feeling of contentment or pleasure. Happiness can come in the form of a person, place, or thing. Believe it or not, happiness is the one thing that people overlook the most and wonder why their passion and purpose is not enough to live a fulfilling life. Our happiness should be at the center of everything we do, and it is not selfish to consider your happiness before another individual's happiness. Making others feel pleasure and contentment is a beautiful personality trait, but we can find ourselves in a position where we feel that love is always being sent and never received. We must consider our happiness while pursuing our passion and purpose because the journey should be a time of joy, not just a time of hard work and reflection.

We must create time for our happiness and allow it to build overtime. Some of us always have the excuse of never having time for ourselves and what makes us happy. When was the last time you did something for yourself? How much time did you spend on yourself? Now think about the amount of time and effort you spent on someone else because you wanted to ensure they were happy. As most of us will realize, we put more effort into other people than ourselves.

During my health recovery journey, I wanted to focus on my mental and emotional health to figure out what triggered my depression. For a certain period, I believed the source of my depression was being cheated on, and that I failed to live up to the expectations of those who loved me dearly. When my health started going in the right direction, I took some time to scroll through my social media pages and reflect on some of the events and programs I was involved in during my college years. I wanted to identify a common trend in every post, comment response, and even text messages to see if I can dig deeper into the cause of my depression. The revelation was that I never did anything that was solely based on my happiness. Most of my posts ended with, "As long I can make other people happy," and my response to a comment or text message would typically be, "I am so happy that I could bring you joy;" when in fact I was not happy at the time. I was not being authentic and social media was my way of producing enough serotonin to make me happy. My need for constant validation was toxic, but I did anything to feel a sense of "happiness" in my life. I understood that I must work on my authenticity and start doing things that make me happy. I understand that you are reading this and might be thinking, "Gio, isn't this selfish?" and my answer is it's not. I put other people in front of my own well-being for way too long and I must put myself first to find peace and happiness of my own.

Some people will try to make you feel guilty for dedicating too much time towards yourself. They feel entitled to tell you that you are "conceited", or not willing to dedicate your time to other people. Truth is, we all dedicate more time to other people than we do ourselves. We care too much about our reputation, and do not realize that we are willing to do anything in order to not end up criticized and alone. My ex-girlfriend tried to place the blame on me for not giving her enough attention and only worrying about my goals and aspirations. I was going to college to build a future for the both of us and all I asked was that she remain loyal and patient. My own peers would say I was too full of myself because I followed up my promises with some action. I learned to protect my happiness and let no one ruin it with their "needs" or simply their desires for me to comply with the social norm. Sometimes, we must just show people that we care for ourselves and that, if we don't, then nobody else will.

Happiness is achieved through the fulfillment of achieving our goals. It is perfectly fine to think about yourself and your well-being. If someone truly loves you, they will be a supporter, not a barrier. We owe absolutely nothing to no one, but we do owe ourselves the happiness we crave.

With everything considered, when was the last time you were truly happy? This question hits deep for a lot of us because we hardly ever reflect on the question. We have so much that is happening in our lives it shifts our focus away from what truly matters to us. We find ways to keep a smile on our faces, but distractions prevent us from claiming our gift. Some people measure their success with the luxuries they own and not by the number of days they spent living happily with their blessings. Life is too short to not put happiness in the center of everything we do. Happiness is not some made up fallacy that only occurs in movies and books. Happiness can be achieved if the person who wants to feel it is willing to fight for it. Think about the people with whom you interact. I bet you $100 that you know more people who are upset with their lives vs. those who are truly happy with how their lives are going. Why choose to be miserable when creating your own happiness is possible? Reflect on this for a moment before you continue the rest of this chapter. We have complete control of our pursuit of happiness and now it is time for you to take control. Sure, go the rest of your life trying to please other people, but see where that leads you when you recognize that your time is cut short and that opportunities have become limited. Go out there and be happy, you don't need anyone's permission to do that.

Happiness is not impossible to achieve and a life without it is not worth living. Happiness is something we all crave and want to pursue. It is the reason why we want to break free from our reality and be in our "happy place". As I said before, we do not need permission from anyone to be happy, but we must work on allowing ourselves to be happy. What I mean by this is that we can work on our happiness through self-care, but we do not take advantage of those moments because we feel we are being selfish with our time. This goes back to my statement made earlier in this chapter where we dedicate more time and effort into things rather than focusing on our own happiness. Happiness should be at the center of everything we do with the reason being that we do not know when our final day is going to be. Now, I would hate to wake up in the morning doing something that does not bring me joy. Not knowing when my final moment is going to be only gives me the motivation to ensure that I take more risks and dedicate more time into things that bring me joy.

This reminds me of the time when I was a Community Assistant (known as a residential assistant) during my undergrad and let me tell you, this was hands down the worst job I ever had. The staff I worked with was amazing, I just didn't enjoy the limited amount of freedom we had as employees, and the established "professional development" initiative that required us to attend events with our residents. In my opinion, these programs were required for us to attend because they were poorly attended in the past and the Housing department continues to pour money into programing that is not working. (That is not the point I am trying to make here; I am just venting my frustrations.) Do not let this discourage you from working in Res-life during college, everyone has a different experience. Getting back to my point, I planned a day for me to just relax, enjoy my favorite foods, and attend a pro-wrestling event that was going to take place in Allentown, PA. I was not scheduled to work the night in my dorm building and I pretty much took the day to focus on my happiness. It was already near the end of the semester and not much was happening on campus for us to be concerned about. On the morning I planned to treat myself, I received an email from my supervisor of the tasks I needed to complete by the end of the day. I asked my supervisor why I was not given these tasks in advance as I already had a day planned for myself. They told me I had no choice but to do it or I would get written up. This is the moment where I had to stand up for myself and do what I had planned for myself, since I had been working hard and my mental health was not good.

I disregarded the tasks in the email and went on with my planned day. It was the best day I had ever experienced during my undergrad. I even made a trip to visit some family before the wrestling event. The next day, I received an email from my supervisor stating I would be written up for refusing to do the tasks that were assigned. I honestly did not care because I wanted to do what made me happy and not let anyone think they had control over that. Now before you say, "This is completely unprofessional Giovanni," understand that I was doing what was best for me and those assigned tasks I was given were for my supervisor to complete, not me. They were trying to pull a fast one by making me feel like I needed to do it, knowing that the jobs were assigned by their director.

I share this story because there will be times in life when we must choose our happiness over anything that does not relate to it. There will be people who will not take your well-being into consideration and will make you feel obligated to fulfill their needs before your own. My decision to pursue my happiness was never a question of my professionalism. Can you think of a time when you were put into a situation like this? How did that make you feel? Did you make the right choice? Our craving for happiness can make us do things of which we are not necessarily proud. I did not want to refuse the direct orders of my supervisor, but they put themselves before me and I did not respect that. Our craving for happiness can force us out of comfort zone so that we can experience something new and exciting.

There was a time when my colleague's PTO request was denied during the slowest time in their office and when my colleague asked why it was denied, his supervisor said, "You cannot expect me to be okay with you taking a vacation with your family while we are stuck here working." My colleague simply responded, "I promised my family and myself this time off and I plan on taking a vacation with your permission or not." He did not return to work and had the most amazing time during his vacation. Again, we must choose our happiness over anything that does not relate to it. My colleague could have simply accepted his supervisor's answer and not gone on a vacation with his family, but he knew how short life can be and that there may not be many chances to connect with his family again. My colleague chose his happiness and pride over a job that did not value his family or his contractually obligated personal time off.

You may not agree with everything that was said in this chapter and that is okay. How you plan to achieve your happiness is completely up to you. What I wanted you to take away in this chapter is that, with your passion and purpose, happiness should be at the center of everything you do. Our happiness should be a top priority and should not be seen as this impossible goal that only the elite can achieve. Remember that some of the poorest individuals in the world live the happiest lives because they value the experiences they encounter and were given another day to live. Give yourself a reason to live a happy life without any interference. People, money, and material can all be replaced overtime. What cannot be replaced is your happiness and the time you spend in this world. Again, none of us know how long we are expected to be in this world. Just make sure to have the time of your life and make sure you are happy at the end of it.

Reflection time:

Are you happy? Why or why not? What can you do to ensure that you can remain or become happy? When is the last time you did something for yourself, and it did not benefit anyone else?

Chapter 6:

Gifting Yourself a Legacy

I personally believe that everyone is blessed with a gift. Some of us are born to create and others are born to serve. Regardless of what we do, our gift is what we do best with the least amount of effort. We are conditioned to believe that we must accept a career that has more prestige in society. The truth is there is nothing more valuable than the gift you possess. Some people ignore their gift because they want the gift of another person. Your gift belongs to you for a reason, and it is because you can do this certain thing better than anyone else could. Our passion and purpose do not only guide us, but they ensure that we are living in our gift. No matter how you feel about yourself currently, we must accept that we deserve to live in our gift. The issue is we run away from our gift because we don't believe we deserve it, and we believe it will not provide us the lifestyle that some of us desire. We become doubtful of our abilities and fold under pressure when things get tough. Being gifted at something is a sign that most people overlook because they believe it is some coincidence that they happen to be good at something. We must stop being so harsh on ourselves and embrace the gift with which we were blessed. It is okay to revisit your past and dust off your gift. Your passion and purpose will always guide you back to it, even when you believe that you are not deserving of it.

A close friend of mine was gifted with the singing voice of an angel. No matter where my friend goes, she will sing at the top of her lungs, and no one will tell her to stop because they are content with her singing ability. My friend's dream was to become a singer and travel around the world. I always encouraged her to pursue her dream, but she did not believe her dream would provide her the lifestyle she desired for herself. Her parents wanted her to become a medical doctor and she eventually believed that to be true as well. My friend struggled to keep up with her classes and barely passed the exams to earn her medical certifications. Over the years, I noticed that she was no longer singing, and her career choice was draining her. I was aware of how rigorous the medical field can be, but it was obvious my friend was miserable. I was hesitant at first, but I had to ask her, "Why are you no longer singing?" I believe it was her first time realizing she was not living in her gift because she began to cry. The next day, I invited her to come with me to a restaurant for their wing night. She loved chicken wings and I thought it would help her destress for a bit. I purposely invited her to this wing night because the restaurant was also hosting a karaoke night. To my amazement, no one volunteered to sing, not even my friend. It wasn't until my friend's favorite song started playing that she closed her eyes and the words started to flow out of her mouth. The people in the restaurant became quiet and all you could hear was her beautiful voice. She sang her heart out and when she finished singing, the people cheered her on and she continued to sing the night away. A couple of weeks after that night, she dropped out of medical school and pursued her dream of becoming a singer.

Now she is paid to sing and gets to travel around the country to perform. She is not making the money that a medical doctor would, but she is happy to be living in her gift. The point of this story is to show that we should claim our gifts because it brings us the most joy and requires the least amount of effort. Why quit something that you are talented at? Stop trying to be something that you are not and continuing a journey that is making you miserable. Some people are gifted to be in the medical field, but some are not, and it is okay to admit that you are not gifted at something. Some of us enjoy being comfortable and following a path that has already been walked on so many times. Just know being comfortable can prevent you from pursuing what you should be doing. You are probably asking right now, "Giovanni, how do you know that you are living in your gift?" You know you are living in your gift when your alarm clock goes off in the morning and it is not a burden to get up. Living in your gift is when your career becomes a lifestyle and is no longer seen as a job. Where money is not the top priority, but you understand that it is a necessity to support yourself and the ones you care for. Do what you are gifted at and stop running away from your gift! Seriously, stop telling yourself that you do not deserve it because there are already people in this world that are going to tell you that, as if they are getting paid to do it. Claim your gift and be the superstar you are destined to become!

My father often said, "Some of us never like to run, but somehow we run away from our blessings." What my father was trying to say is that we do not believe we deserve the blessings we pray for when the time is right. As humans, I believe we are too harsh and critical of ourselves. We force ourselves to believe that we do not deserve great things because of certain mistakes we committed or trauma we experienced growing up. It is easy for me to tell you to claim your gift, but I understand that not everyone can do so because of mental, emotional, or physical barriers. However, I believe we deserve to live in our gift despite the setbacks we encounter. Accepting your gift involves looking past your flaws. Believe it or not, our flaws are what make us unique, and no one ever said we cannot turn our flaws into our best features.

    We simply cannot run from our gift forever. There will be a time when you will feel as if you have been held back for too long and will no longer allow it. You truly think you are not gifted? Then why did someone ask you to develop a logo for them? Out of all the music producers in the nation, why did they ask you to create an intro for them? Why did someone reach out to you and ask if you can share you story for the book they are writing? The answer to that is that you are gifted, and the world is waiting for you to allow us to appreciate and compensate you for your gifts. Do not be average when you know deep down that you are great! Greatness is instilled in everyone, and it is your choice what you decide to do with it. Just because your family, friends, or colleagues did not use their gifts does not make you incapable of using your own. We are tasked with the responsibility of creating a legacy by which we will be remembered. The validation we are craving now will not even matter once we are buried six feet under. It is the legacy that we leave behind that everyone will talk about.

Legacy is forever evolving and the one thing that continues to open doors for the new generation of dreamers and movers. It is your gifts that will allow other people to believe in themselves. Understanding and internalizing your gifts does not only make you great, but a role model to those who are seeking guidance and mentorship. We cannot be afraid to gift ourselves a legacy that will be respected while being alive and respected for decades after we die. Therefore, it is so important for us to stop running away from our gift. Accepting your gifts does not only benefit you, but it can also create a positive impact on one individual or even an entire community! We need your gifts more than ever and I believe not accepting them is the biggest wrong you can commit against yourself. You may not care about what people will think about you after you are gone but understand that you can be a hero to someone else and they will forever be grateful for you. Stop running away from your gift. We may not love to run, but we will certainly run away when something great is presented to us. My father did not tell me this because he wanted me to be average, he wanted me to give back to the world through my gifts and be remembered for it.

My legacy was established during the 2021 PA Latino Convention in Reading, PA. I finally returned to my hometown from grad school, and I was excited to launch the inaugural Legacy Summit during the convention. The Legacy Summit was organized by college students and created for other college students to attend, providing them an opportunity to network and facilitate workshops on their own. Not only was I excited for this, but I was given an opportunity to speak during our annual Hispanic Heritage gala. I crafted a speech that addressed reclaiming my health and the status of the young professionals in Pennsylvania. Days before the convention, I provided a copy of my speech to my mentor and had him look it over for grammatical errors. He looked at me and said, "Giovanni, this is great, but this is not the speech you want to give." With confusion, I asked, "Why?" and my mentor went on to tell me something that changed my life forever. He placed both his hands on my shoulders, looked me directly in the eyes, and said, "Giovanni, you are gifted with the ability to speak your truth and this speech is lacking authenticity. Use this opportunity to open doors for other people, not for yourself." At first, I believed their feedback was insulting, but then I realized that the speech was more about me and not about being a voice for young people. I knew that, at the gala, I had to use my gift and be the voice of the young professional who has been overlooked, undervalued, and underrepresented.

The room was filled with elected officials, business owners, influencers, and people of power. It was my turn to speak, and I started to speak my part about reclaiming my health, after that, I let those people have it. The line that hit some the hardest was, "Young professionals are not stepping up for the photo op. We entrusted some of you to be our progressive guides. We had to step up because some of you did not understand the assignment." After my speech, I was given a standing ovation and positive feedback from the audience. The speech certainly burned bridges for me, but it ignited a fire within the young professionals that night and I fulfilled my mission.

I used my gift to create a legacy and forever will be remembered as the man who stood up for young professionals. We cannot be afraid to step out of our comfort zones and burn bridges. Our gifts make the world a better place and encourage others to never be afraid to use their own gifts. Comfort is what makes us stagnant, and your gift will make you uncomfortable until you create a legacy of your own. Your gift will always belong to you, and I encourage you not to waste it just so that you can remain comfortable with being average.

Reflection Time:

What do you want your legacy to be? Does it relate to your passion and purpose? Will this make you happy? Do you believe your legacy will be respected and appreciated while you are still here? Will this legacy be appreciated and valued by generations after you?

Chapter 7:

Claim Your Glory Without Fear

We all experience fear at different points in our lives and, for some, it controls the way we travel during our journey. Fear is a collection of uncertainty, anxiety, and insecurities that builds overtime and creates a burden in someone's development. Fear is an inevitable part of life that we wish never occurred, but unfortunately, we all fall victim to it when making decisions that can potentially change our lives for the better. Fear follows us wherever we go and there seems to be no way to escape it. We are constantly reminded of our fears in different forms, such as nightmares or sudden panic attacks. It is very courageous for someone to say, "I fear nothing," but it does not make them any stronger than the person who constantly lives in fear. Being fearful is completely normal, but letting it run your life is a major problem that should be addressed. This may be hard to digest for some, however fear is nothing but an illusion.

If you look up the definition of illusion, you can see that it is defined as a false idea or belief. You're not scared of what you can potentially do, but you are fearful that you are going to fail. The reason that is a false idea is because you probably never tried, or you just do not know where to start. If you give yourself every reason to believe that you are going to fail, then chances are you will. Fear is an illusion our mind tricks us into believing because it triggers those parts of our brains that store our insecurities and self-doubt. As someone who is looking to unlock their passion, purpose, and happiness, we must address these fears head on and prove these fears to be false beliefs. Looking at the development stages between childhood and adulthood, there are so many things we initially thought were impossible to achieve and yet, somehow, we prevailed at the end. My parents often like to say, "We fear of what we don't know is possible, but with patience and practice, we can do anything we put our minds to," and I agree with this statement because we do not become aware of what we are capable until we take the first step.

I once worked for a grocery store and applied to be a grocery stocker with no desire of ever becoming a cashier. I did not believe I would be a good cashier considering I was never a cashier before and the pace in which a cashier must move gave me anxiety. My job was experiencing a staff shortage and the employees who remained were being asked to take on multiple responsibilities beyond their job descriptions. My supervisor told me that I would have to begin cashier training right away and I was petrified. What if I screwed up? What if I miscounted my money drawer? What if a customer begins to yell at me and I cannot keep my composure? So many questions began to run through my head, and I was fearful of doing a bad job. I literally almost quit my job, but I did not want to cause a strain on my supervisor because the store was already short staffed. Instead of running away, I stepped up and took on the challenge. My first day as a cashier went horribly, but I realized I made a breakthrough by trying it out before quitting. As the weeks progressed, I got so much better at being a cashier that my fear was gone. I gained a new skill that I initially believed was never going to happen and all I had to do was take the first step.

I'm sure many of us had to overcome a fear, whether it was riding a roller-coaster to conquer your fear of heights or getting your driver's license to overcome your fear of driving. Whatever the case may be, it is important to take the steps necessary to overcome fear. Fear prevents us from doing many things in life that enable us to build upon our passion, purpose, and happiness. It even prevents us from claiming our gifts and using them for a great cause.

Fear should not run your life because it is simply a skill or knowledge you have not acquired yet.

As mentioned before, fear can come in many forms; and an overlooked fear is going through your journey alone. I know I said that we can't be dependent of other people when it comes to our goals, but there is nothing wrong with wanting a support system. Not having a strong support system can cause uncertainty and, worst-case scenario, severe depression. No one wants to be successful and not have anyone with whom to celebrate that success. We all want love, support, and attention during our journey so that we know we are on the right track and can say that at least one person is proud. In some cases, those things are not available, and some people must depend on themselves and hope they don't burnout from the lack of affection and appreciation.

Overcoming the fear of being alone may not be such an easy task for everyone. Some people can't trust others who lack consistency and set up a defensive barrier to whomever can't meet their standards. Setting personal barriers is good in the sense of making sure no one takes advantage of you but blocking every single person out may not be healthy. I say that because not everyone is at the same level as you, but they can be the best source of support and love that we need to succeed. Overcoming this fear will require you to make connections and set reasonable boundaries with the people you are allowing into your life. I am saying this from personal experience, please do not be that person who believes that everything must be done on their own and that they will not find love and support. You may feel this way because you seek love and support from the people you grew up with, but the moment you experience rejection from these people, the fear of being alone starts to kick in. Understand that love and support is everywhere if you seek it in the right places and I promise you that there will be people who will be there to appreciate your gifts.

After my last relationship ended, I realized quickly that I lost touch with a lot of people. I really had no one to turn to so that I can vent my feelings and other stressors that were bringing me down. I would try to reach out to people that were close to me and my messages would just be ignored. My worst fear was coming true and that was the fear of walking my journey alone. My siblings were focused on their personal lives and relationships, so I did not want to be a bother to them. My parents are my only trusted source of support but telling them my issues was no easy task. I would constantly tell myself, "I don't need anyone, I can do this all on my own," and it did not phase me until I started feeling like I was a ghost. I would enter a room and there would be no reaction. Nobody seemed to be worried about my whereabouts and my overall health. Days, weeks, and even months would go by and not a single person would offer to hang out or even check in with me. I began to ask myself if I was a bad person and if people just had enough of me. I felt like I was no longer accepted by the people I grew up with and was rejected by my own hometown. I was even experiencing this at college, and it made me feel horrible. Unfortunately, I entered a stage of my life where I closed myself off to the world and just accepted the fact that I am alone.

Once I reclaimed my health and graduated from Kutztown University, I decided to pursue my master's degree at Indiana University of PA and give myself a "fresh start". You may be asking, "How is leaving your hometown going to make you feel less alone?" and truth is that being home caused me to become stagnant and I needed to reinvent myself. I became too comfortable with being alone and only depended on the support of the people I grew up with. I made the move to introduce myself to new people and give myself a chance to grow in a new environment.

Overtime, I made new connections and gained the support of people I never encountered before. I even challenged myself to do things I never did before, like participating in a Halloween costume contest! It became clear that my fear of being alone was all in my head. I was loved, supported, and appreciated by many and I just needed to seek it in places I have never been before.

Now to address the biggest fear of them all and that is the fear of failure. There is no worse feeling than knowing you are not doing enough to fulfill your passion and purpose. The fear of failure is the reason so many refuse to transform their dreams into careers. This fear causes people to overwork themselves to a point of desperation and misery. As stated earlier in this chapter, if you believe you are going to fail, the chances are that you will. The best way to address this fear is to accept that failure enhances growth and success. The truth is that failure is inevitable when pursuing our dreams. We should aim to create teachable moments when making and taking on a new goal. Everyone views failure in a different way, but it can be perceived as an opportunity to reflect on what went wrong and what can be improved by the next time an opportunity presents itself. Being scared to fail is not uncommon because it is a universal fear that people share all over the world. We all want to be successful at what we are passionate about and some just cannot deal with the fact that their success is not guaranteed. Success is guaranteed when we learn, adapt, and execute on the action steps we set for ourselves to make sure we reach our goals.

Failure can cause people to act out and do things that are not ethical. I remember the time my former colleague earned a promotion at their job, and it came with many benefits, such as a huge pay raise and new car. I was happy for them at the time because they really wanted the promotion and the prestige that came with the promotion. Unfortunately, it was later revealed that they had blackmailed the other candidates and had a romantic affair with the supervisor. An investigation was launched, and my former colleague was immediately fired. This individual's fear of not getting the promotion caused them to become desperate and commit some unethical acts to ensure their success. This person ruined their entire career just for an opportunity that could have been available at another job site.

The reason I share this with you is because we should never sell out to our fears. Yes, losing out on opportunities can make us question why we do things ethically, but understand the damage that can be caused by doing the wrong thing. If you are a believer in your passion and purpose, then you know that your gifts will take you where you want to go. There is no need to commit unethical acts to get where you want to be. There is simply no reward in it, and it will only come back to haunt you in the end. My former colleague believed their life was set for themselves, but eventually lost everything, including their money and family. There will be times in which we really want something and know it will be a tough process to earn it. Please take my advice and trust the process! If you fail during your pursuit, then just work on ways you can improve. Do not find ways to cheat the process and end up with nothing in the end.

How you decide to control your fear will determine the level of success you will achieve. Fear is only knowledge or skills you have not yet acquired, so please do not feel you are not capable of doing anything. Fear is guaranteed to make you feel uncomfortable but will push you to take on new challenges and become stronger in the process. Our fears must be approached with a positive attitude and hard work ethic. Do not cover up your fears with bad decisions because it will only show that you are weak and will fold under pressure. Fear is only preventing you from becoming the person you were born to be. Never let fear control your passion, purpose, and happiness!

Falling off your path and having to reinvent yourself is not easy. To claim our glory, we must constantly remind ourselves why our dreams matter. You must be prepared to do whatever it takes to reach your destination. This includes sleepless nights, lonely days, and having a few dollars to your name. Certain events or people will make you feel as if you are not doing enough. Claiming your glory is not as easy as it sounds. I wish I could tell you that it is a linear process. You are going to encounter multiple challenges during your journey to glory. These challenges will become too much to handle, and the burnout will make you question if your dream is worth pursuing. There is no glory if you do not fight for what you desire in life.

Claiming your glory involves applying pressure to yourself and internalizing the commitment made to your passion and purpose. Applying pressure means that you are ready to start producing diamonds and will not fold when tough times arise. This means that you will need to remove the excuses out of your life and find time for your dreams. This life stage requires you to make sacrifices and put yourself in places you have never been before. You must manifest your glory before it even occurs so that you are aware of what you are fighting for. You are not owed anything in this world, so do not even think about placing blame on anyone as to why you didn't achieve glory. Claiming your glory is a privilege that some do not take seriously, and they lose it because they do not appreciate it enough. Your glory reflects your passion, purpose, and happiness; and, if glory is not achieved, those three things will become useless.

Earlier in this book, I told the story about reclaiming my health so that I can pursue my dreams and fulfill my promises. There was another reason why I wanted to reclaim my health and that was to fall in love. I had this great plan to marry the woman of my dreams and become a father. My love life has not been great considering I have been rejected because of my weight and the one time I did find love; I was cheated on. I would pray for love to find its way to me, and I would become angry when women would not give me a chance. After I got bariatric sleeve surgery and lost weight, I believed it was finally time for women to take interest in me and that did not happen at all. I waved my fist angrily in the air and asked why I could not be loved after all I have put myself through to be alive. Then, I soon realized that I did find love and that love came in the form of the sacrifices I had to make for my dreams to come true.

When claiming your glory, we must make sense of why things we desire come in different forms. I wanted to be in love with another woman and instead I was given the strength to find self-love to fix my wrongs. The reason our desires come in different forms is because we must learn to appreciate what we have and what we can handle during certain points of our lives. We mistake being ready with being confident and we must humble ourselves before our glory can be claimed. We cannot enter our glory days thinking all our problems have been resolved because of the success that was achieved. We must work on ourselves and our overall health to ensure our glory days can be lived with peace and happiness. Claiming your glory is not about making a lot of money and reaching the top, it is truly about finding fulfillment and knowing that your dream was worth fighting for.

    I am sure that we all heard the saying, "If you fall down, then you must get right back up," and this saying is true when it comes to claiming your glory. Some people do not get back up because they are afraid to fall again. Their fall caused such an inconvenience in their lives that they decided to remain grounded. These are the type of people who become complacent because they preferred to remain stagnant. Chasing your dreams is going to come with bumps, bruises, and scars. These marks will symbolize your commitment and strength towards fulfilling your goals. The reality is that if you don't summon the courage to get back up, don't expect anyone or anything to lift you up. This responsibility falls solely on you and do not dare blame the world for your misfortunes. Understand that everything we do involves making a choice and the convenient option is not always the best. When claiming your glory, you will have to fight until your dream becomes a reality.

We all experience disappointing times in our lives and those moments should not limit your drive for success. I've been ignored, teased, humiliated, threatened, betrayed, and even told to kill myself in order to see my dreams flourish. To be honest, I am very grateful to have encountered all those misfortunes because I would not be where I am without them. There are going to be certain life events or people who are going to limit your potential and I say let these experiences bring the fight out of you. Do not let these things bring fear and insecurity into your life because there is glory that needs to be claimed. Do not stop dreaming because someone else is scared to claim their glory. Go start that business and become a millionaire. Take that flight to Germany and start a new life. If dropping out of college is going to allow you to pursue your passion and purpose full time, please take that leap of faith and do not let anyone's judgement of you stop you from doing it. We owe nothing to no one, and the journey belongs to you!

Allow me to share my final thoughts with you. We only have one life to make things great for ourselves and we unfortunately don't know when that time will come to an end. Your passion, purpose, and pursuit of happiness are the 3 tools that will allow you to live the life you want. We have become accustomed to living a life where we have to follow a path that has already been paved. We are not obligated to follow that path and have every right to pave our own. Choosing this path will come with a lot of criticism, judgement, and hate that will come from people who do not like you or who are too afraid to take a leap of faith. Prove to yourself that you are a believer in what you do and claim your glory at all costs. Remain open-minded and do not be fearful of the changes that occur during your journey. Now it is time for you to set yourself free and be the author of your own story. I believe in you and wish you the best of luck in your future endeavors. Now, go out and go inspire others with your passion, purpose, and happiness!

Final reflection:

What are your insecurities? What are you fearful of? Who is a part of your support system? Are they contributing to your passion, purpose, and pursuit of happiness? Do you believe in your dream? Will you claim your glory? What steps are necessary for you to achieve your dream?

About the Author

Giovanni Negron-Garcia is the CEO and Owner of GioEffect Life Coaching and Public Speaking, LLC. Giovanni is born and raised in Reading, PA, a city that is defined by crime, poverty, and corruption. Giovanni is caring, ambitious, and energetic. Throughout his journey, Giovanni encountered numerous battles with his mental and physical health. He reached the weight of 366 lbs., which set the course of ending his life by the age of 35. Through discipline and soul searching, Giovanni reclaimed his health and lost over 200 lbs. in less than a year! Giovanni claims that he had to redefine his passion and purpose, so that he can share his gifts with the world and claim the glory he almost lost. Now, he has become an inspiration around the nation, as he displays his message of, "Go. Inspire. Others". Giovanni believes that everyone has a gift to share with the world and that will contribute to their legacy. Giovanni Negron-Garcia helps underprivileged professionals achieve their goals and dreams based on their career aspirations.

Made in the USA
Monee, IL
25 February 2022